LIVEWIRE
INVESTIGATES

KU-521-417

Being a Model

Iris Howden

Published in association with The Basic Skills Agency

Hodder & Stoughton
A MEMBER OF THE HODDER HEADLINE GROUP

Acknowledgements

Cover: Naomi Campbell, Corbis/AFP.

Photos: © Corbis pp. 3, 19; PA News Photo Library pp. 7, 11, 21, 24, 27; The Ronald Grant Archive p. 15

Orders: please contact Bookpoint Ltd, 130 Milton Park, Abingdon, Oxon OX14 4SB. Telephone: (44) 01235 400414. Fax: (44) 01235 400454. Lines are open from 9.00–6.00, Monday to Saturday, with a 24-hour message answering service. Email address: orders@bookpoint.co.uk

British Library Cataloguing in Publication Data
A catalogue record for this title is available from The British Library

ISBN 0 340 74716 1

First published 1999
Impression number   10 9 8 7 6 5 4 3 2
Year   2004 2003 2002 2001

Typeset by Fakenham Photosetting Ltd, Fakenham, Norfolk.
Printed in Great Britain for Hodder & Stoughton Educational, a division of Hodder Headline Plc, 338 Euston Road, London NW1 3BH by The Bath Press, Bath

Contents

The Interview

Sally is a reporter for her school magazine.
She has set up a meeting with Zoe, a model.
She goes to meet Zoe at a hotel in town.
Sally has a list of questions to ask her.

Zoe   Hi Sally.
Nice to meet you.
I've had some coffee brought up.

Sally   Thanks a lot.

Zoe   Did you find the hotel OK?

Sally   Yes, my dad gave me a lift.

Zoe   Right, let's get started.
So, you want to interview me
for your school magazine?

Sally   Yes, I've brought a copy
for you to look at.

Zoe   This looks great.
Really professional.

Sally Thanks. It's a joint effort –
students and staff.
One of the teachers
is into desk-top publishing.
Lots of the kids
write about their hobbies:
sport, pop music and so on.
I want to be a journalist
when I leave school
so I've done quite a few interviews.
Do you mind if I use a tape recorder?

Zoe Not at all.
Fire away.

Sally This is a list of questions
some of the others want me to ask you.
One or two girls are keen
to know more about modelling.
Some of the lads are too.

Zoe Go ahead.
I'll do my best to answer them.

Sally Vicky wonders
if it's worth staying on at school.
She says she plans to hang around
at places like the Clothes Show Live.
She's hoping a scout will spot her.

Kate Moss started modelling very young.

Zoe	She should be so lucky!
	I don't think that's very likely.
	It's true, scouts do look out
	for new models.
	We all know about Kate Moss
	being spotted by the STORM agency.
	She was standing in a queue
	at the JFK Airport.
	But it doesn't happen very often.

Sally	The very young models
	have usually been spotted,
	haven't they?
	I read about one who was only 12.

Zoe	True, but she had to go
	and work abroad.
	She got a lot of flak
	from the British press.
	Young female models
	are always in demand.
	It all started
	with Twiggy in the 1960s.
	I know of a few 14 and 15 year olds.
	But I'm not sure it's a good idea.
	Some of the older models resent them.
	They're often asked to wear clothes
	that are much too old for them.
	Or do things they're not happy with.

| | The main thing, if you are under 16, |
| | is to take someone with you. |

The main thing, if you are under 16,
is to take someone with you.
And don't sign any contract.
Get a parent or an older friend
to read it first.

Sally   How old were you when you started?

Zoe   I was 17.
My parents wanted me to take
my GCSE exams first.
I'm glad I did now.
Modelling's a very short career
– and a very chancy one.
You need something to fall back on.
Boys can do better than girls
in this job.
They have a longer working life.
There's much more work
for older male models.

Sally   Sushila wants to know
if there are any modelling courses
you can take at college.

Zoe   As far as I know
there's only one state college
that offers a course in modelling.
That's the London College of Fashion.
It's a one year full-time course.
You need to be 16 to apply.

Sally   Do you need good exam results
to get in?

Zoe   I think they want three GCSEs at grade C.
Modelling's one of the few jobs
where you don't need
paper qualifications.

Sally   How did you get started?

Zoe   I did a course
at a private modelling school in London.
You need to make sure it's a good one.
Some of them cheat young people.
They take them on just to get the fees.
It's better to find one
that will be honest
about your chance of success.

Models have to learn how to move.

Sally	Did you enjoy the course?
	What sort of things did you learn?

Zoe	I loved it.
	We learned all sorts of things.
	How to move.
	How to walk down a cat walk.
	How to wear clothes.
	How to pose for the camera.
	There are some courses for people
	who aren't planning to be models.
	They teach you
	how to make the best of yourself.
	One of those could be useful for you,
	if you wanted to go in for TV reporting.
	They give you confidence.
	Next question.

Sally	Paul wants to know how you go about
	finding work as a model.

Zoe	Well, the school teaches you the basics.
	Then you have to do the round of agents
	until you find one willing to take you on.
	Again, make sure he or she is genuine.
	You can send off
	for a list of good agents.
	Once you've signed with an agency,
	they find you work.
	The agent takes part of your fee
	for each job.

Sally   Was it easy to find an agent?

Zoe   Not really.
           It took a while.
           One or two turned me down.
           But I didn't give up hope.
           The agent who took me on
           was very fair.
           She said I had a good chance
           of being a model.
           I was tall enough.
           You have to be at least 5 foot 8.
           And I've got a good, slim figure;
           a dress size 10.
           She liked my straight nose,
           and good cheek bones.
           But she thought
           I should get my teeth fixed.
           She also said
           I should work out in the gym.
           It would help to keep my body toned.

Sally   I'm surprised she said all that.
           I think you're really pretty.

Zoe   Thanks, but being pretty isn't enough.
There are thousands
of pretty girls around.
They don't all make it.
These days you stand more chance
if your looks are a bit unusual.
Some models from an ethnic mix do well.
And now that girl power is all the rage
there's a call for what they call 'attitude'.
You have to act for the camera.

Sally   What about boys?
Is it the same for them.

Zoe   Boys have to be taller –
5 foot 11 at least.
They don't have to be
all that good looking.
If they're tall and thin
with a strong jaw
and good bones, that's fine.
Some boys don't enjoy
all the hanging around.
They tend to get bored.
They want more action.

Boys should be tall and thin.

Sally   Is it boring, then?

Zoe   It can be.
You often spend ages
waiting to have your hair
or your make-up done.
A photographer may go off
and leave you standing about
while he does something else.

Sally   Did your agent
get you a job right away?

Zoe   It's not that simple.
Getting taken on by an agent is
only the first step.
You have to have a 'book'
of your photos made up.
This shows the different ways
you can look.
It can cost quite a lot.
You take it with you
when you go on interviews
and show it to the clients.
There are often lots of models
being tested for the same job.

You might not be chosen that day.
But you mustn't take it to heart.
They may be looking
for a different type.
Don't forget,
the agent can find you work.
It's up to you
to make sure you get the job.
Take a deep breath
and smile as you go in.
Try to look confident,
even if you don't feel it.
And learn to cope
with being turned down.

Sally   What was your first job?

Zoe   I was taken on as a house model.
It was for a firm
that made teenage fashions.
I had to show the clothes off
to the buyers.
It wasn't very well paid
but it was good experience.
I learned a lot about the fashion trade.
I did that for a year.
I did some freelance work too.
My goal was
to be a photographic model.

Sally   Did you get a thrill seeing your photo
in all the glossy magazines?

Zoe   That didn't happen until much later.
And yes,
it was a thrill when I made *Vogue*.
But I'd spent
some time getting known.
My first fashion shoot
was for a catalogue.
A lot of famous people start that way:
doing catalogue work
or knitting patterns.
The film star Roger Moore for one.
Some models never move out of this area.
A girl can make a living modelling tights
if she's got good legs.
Or nail varnish
if she's got pretty hands.
Models are used to sell lots of products:
electrical goods, cars,
food, make-up etc.
A lot of guys are used
to advertise beer.

Jeremy Irons once advertised beer.

Sally	Dina wants to know
	what the pay is like.
	What sort of money
	does a model make?

Zoe	It all depends on what the job is,
	and how well known you are.
	We hear about the vast sums
	top models get.
	They're the lucky few.
	It's hard going at first.
	You need money for your course
	and your book of photos.
	You need enough to keep yourself
	until your career takes off.
	You also have to buy a lot of things
	to carry around from job to job.
	Different shoes, tights, make-up etc.
	I've been lucky.
	I've made a steady income.
	More than I would have got in most jobs.
	I've always been able to pay the rent
	and save a bit as well.
	You only have a few years as a model.
	I want to have some money put by
	for when I finish.

Sally	What will you do then?
Zoe	I'm not sure.
	Something in the fashion world.
	I'd like to own a dress shop one day.
	I may get married and have kids.
	My boyfriend wants to.
	He's a photographer
	so he understands the way I live.
	We don't see all that much of each other.
	Either I'm away or he is.
	It can be very tiring,
	rushing about from job to job.
	The one thing you do need as a model
	is plenty of sleep.
Sally	That leads on to my next question.
	Jill wants to know if there are any
	special beauty routines you follow.
Zoe	Well, I do take good care of my skin.
	Heavy make-up can ruin it.
	I make sure I cleanse it really well
	before I go to bed.
	And I drink plenty of water.
	That helps to keep it clear.
	A spot can be a major disaster.

Sally	Do you follow any special diet?

Zoe

Not really.
I just try to eat a normal healthy diet.
I eat plenty of fruit and vegetables every day.
I like fish and chicken, bread and pasta.
I avoid eating too many fatty foods –
like chips.
A treat like chocolate is OK
once in a while – but not all the time.
And I hardly ever drink alcohol.

Sally

You must be very strong willed.
Meeta wants to travel.
She asks if you get much chance
to do that as a model.

Zoe

That's one of the perks of the job.
I've been all over the world.
Fashion shoots are often in exotic places.
Mind you, it's not all as glam as it looks.
Clothes are brought out
six months in advance.
You can be modelling a bikini in winter
or thick woolly jumpers in a heat wave.
Photos have to be taken in good light.
That means getting up really early.
Often it's five in the morning.
But we do have some fun abroad too.
I've made lots of good friends.

A fashion shoot on the beach.

Sally	I wanted to ask you about that.
	You hear of models going around together.
	Jerry Hall and Marie Helvin
	in their day.
	Naomi Campbell, Kate Moss
	and Claudia Schiffer now.
	Do they really get on so well?
Zoe	You're talking about top names there.
	I don't know many supermodels.
	But yes, they're good friends.
	The top designers use top models.
	They appear in the same shows
	in Paris, New York and Rome.
	They're bound to meet quite often.
	Modelling is a competitive job
	so some girls do fall out.
	There was something in the papers
	not long ago.
	It was a lot of fuss about Naomi Campbell
	and another black model
	called Tyra Banks.
	I think the press blew it up
	because it made a good story.
	Most of the girls get on really well.
	We have a good laugh.

Many of the supermodels are good friends.

Sally   You read a lot in the press
about heroin chic or grunge.
How do you feel about that?

Zoe   I hate it.
I'm glad it's going out!
Models want to look good – not ugly.
That look was just a fad but it got publicity
after President Clinton spoke about it.
People began to take notice.
The editor of *Vogue* banned some photos.
She said the rooms the models were in
looked like junkies' dens.
She won't use models who are on drugs.

Sally   What about really skinny models?
A lot of girls at school starve themselves.
They want to look like models.
Do you think fashion pages are to blame?

Zoe   That's a real issue.
Buyers want to see clothes on thin models.
Magazines like to use pictures of them.
But really, there aren't many people
out in the real world, who are that thin!
The pictures can send out
the wrong message to young people.
Anorexia, the slimming disease,
affects quite a few people now –
boys and girls.
But things are starting to change.

Some models have been dropped
because they look too thin.
I read the other day
that doctors want to see
different body types being shown.
They'd like to see some bigger models
like Sophie Dahl
as well as the skinny waifs.

Sally   This question is from Steph.
Her mother's not keen for her to be a model.
She's worried
Steph might pose for sleazy pictures.

Zoe   That shouldn't happen
if she has a good agent.
Tell her not to have anything to do with
one that deals in
so-called 'glamour' pictures.
A model can refuse to do anything
she's not happy about –
such as posing topless.
Some young models pose
for topless calendars.
They regret it later on
when they're better known.
Anything else?

Sophie Dahl.

Sally   A question from Tal.
              She wants to know
              if you can get into acting
              through being a model first.

Zoe   It's not easy.
              Some models have gone on to acting,
              Joanna Lumley for one.
              In her life story she writes about
              her early days in TV.
              She was always the pretty girlfriend.
              She didn't get good parts till she was older.
              One problem is that you must be in Equity,
              the actor's union, to make even an advert.
              Tal would do better to take an acting course.
              Is that the last question?

Sally   No, there's one more.
              It's from Ray.
              He says he quite fancies being a model
              but he thinks a lot of the clothes look daft.
              He saw some photos
              of Men's Fashion Week.
              He says,
              'One guy was wearing what looked like
              a girl's blouse.
              Another had an octopus on his head.
              Can a model refuse to wear things like that?'

Zoe   Oh dear, not really.
You have to remember that designers
want to make the headlines at these shows.
People like Vivienne Westwood
can seem over the top at times.
Not all her clothes are so way out.
And they're fun to wear.
You can't pick and choose what you model.
And you have to enjoy dressing up.
I think Ray had better opt
for another career.

Sally   Thanks so much for giving up your time,
Zoe.
And thanks for letting us use your photo.

Zoe   That's OK Sally, I've enjoyed our chat.
Good luck with the article.
Make sure you send me a copy of it
when the magazine comes out.

Some of the clothes are a bit way out.

Useful Addresses

These are the addresses Zoe talked about.

Don't forget to enclose
a stamped addressed envelope
if you write off for details.

Association of Model Agents
The Clockhouse
St Catherine's Mews
Milner Street
London SW3 PX

London College of Fashion
20 John Prince's Street
London W1M OBJ